KV-578-920

CREATING
GARDEN
POOLS

ALAN TITCHMARSH

CREATING
GARDEN
POOLS

HAMLYN

ACKNOWLEDGEMENTS

Cover photograph by Photos Horticultural
Title page photograph by BBC Enterprises
Colour photographs
Pat Brindley, pages 35, 43, 45; The Daily Telegraph Colour
Library, page 39; John Dawes, page 42; Impact Photos/Pamla
Toler, page 49; David Johnson, page 20; S. & O. Mathews,
page 22–3 (Cobblers, Crowborough); Tania Midgley, page 47;
Photos Horticultural, pages 19, 24, 27; The Harry Smith
Horticultural Photographic Collection, pages 10, 14, 37, 50,
52, 54–5; Uitgeverij Het Spectrum B.V., Utrecht/Amsterdam,
pages 32, 40. Other photographs by Hamlyn Publishing.

This book is based on *Garden Pools* first published in 1984
by The Hamlyn Publishing Group Limited.
This revised edition published in 1986 by Hamlyn Publishing,
Bridge House, London Road, Twickenham, Middlesex, England

Copyright © 1984, 1986 Hamlyn Publishing
a division of The Hamlyn Publishing Group Limited

All rights reserved. No part of this publication may be
reproduced, stored in a retrieval system, or transmitted,
in any form or by any means, electronic, mechanical,
photocopying, recording or otherwise, without the prior
permission of Hamlyn Publishing.

ISBN 0 600 30707 7

Phototypeset in England by Servis Filmsetting Limited
in 10 on 11pt Apollo

Printed in Spain by Cayfosa. Barcelona
Dep. Leg. B-11520-1986

CONTENTS

A shallow stream trickles down a slope over a bed of pebbles to join a circular pool

INTRODUCTION

There's something about the very word. A pool sounds inviting. A pond doesn't. And yet so many gardeners don't bother with water at all, except when it's coming out of the end of a hosepipe. I wonder why?

I reckon that the 'pond' image has a lot to do with it. Flanders and Swann claimed at one time that they were responsible for putting the brass bedsteads into village ponds the length and breadth of the country. Since then the brass bedstead has become fashionable and it's been fished out of ponds to be replaced by a car tyre, a spiral of barbed wire, a supermarket trolley and a left-hand wellington boot. The pond itself seems no more than a breeding ground for mosquito larvae. But the pool is something different.

Whether you're a relaxed gardener or someone who is never still, water can be made to fit into your plot. A flat sheet of water will bring a tranquil air unparalleled by any stretch of lawn, and as well as providing a calming influence, it has reflective qualities that mirror both the sky and the surrounding plants.

Where movement is needed there are fountains and waterfalls to play with. A little caution is advisable here. That feast of fountains you saw in the garden centre will probably look like something out of an Hawaiian ballroom of a holiday camp once you've installed it in your garden. The keynote is simplicity. Some gardens can cope with an elaborate water system but most are better for a single fountain jet or a waterfall that tumbles in a clean sheet over a sharp edge rather than down a watercourse which looks as though it has lost its way to the Lake District.

Where space and funds are short there's no need to forego the pleasure of a pool. Half a beer barrel will do. If garden width is a problem settle for a narrow channel of water bordered by bricks or timber sleepers – formal waterways are most fashionable at the moment.

There is one disadvantage to introducing water to the garden; once it's there you'll never want to be without it.

The Pool for Pleasure

The pool is to the garden what television is to the house – you'll sit staring at it for hours. What's more you'll never tire of the programmes offered by a sheet of limpid water; they change daily and with the seasons offering the best natural history series you've ever seen.

To the gardener, water brings a whole new world of plants – water lilies and flag irises, monkey flowers and fairy floating moss – as well as a mirror that reflects and multiplies the brilliant flowers growing on its banks.

But the real value of water lies in the wildlife it attracts. Whether you like it or not, your pool will act like a magnet to frogs and toads (brilliant controllers of slugs), pond skaters and water snails, newts and water boatmen. Dragonflies and demoiselles, skilled at aerobatics, will cavort over the water flashing their blue, red, or metallic green bodies in the sunlight.

Enough of the romance! How can you build a pool that has all these advantages without the pitfalls of pea-green water and mud?

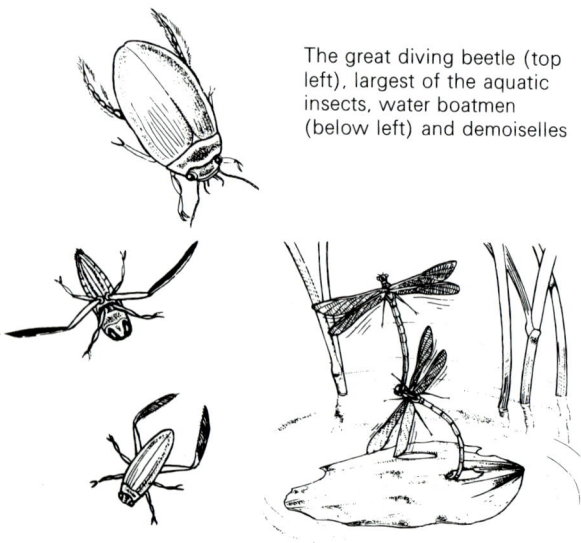

The great diving beetle (top left), largest of the aquatic insects, water boatmen (below left) and demoiselles

A Place for Water

It's no use putting a pool in a dingy corner of the garden overshadowed by a shed and a clump of trees. Pools need bright light if the plants and fish are to thrive and the water is to stay clear. Find a spot that's open to the sky without being exposed to howling winds.

Pools under trees will fill up with autumn leaves which poison the water and the fish. If you simply can't get away from trees you'll have to stretch plastic close-weave netting over the pool in September to catch the leaves.

Without a doubt, the pool will be at its most glamorous between spring and autumn, so position it where it can be enjoyed at that time of the year. Placed right outside your kitchen window it might be just a bit too murky for your liking in the heart of winter.

Shape and size

Make your pool as big as possible. Not only will the water stay clearer, but you'll also have more room to grow a captivating selection of plants. Formal pools may be round, square or rectangular and will suit tidy, formal gardens, but irregular-shaped pools look more natural. Make them bold and sweeping. Don't go in for lots of twiddly bits; they'll look messy.

The best depth for a pool is 45cm (18in). If it is made any shallower than this it will heat up too quickly in summer and rapidly turn into a green broth; what's more, the fish will be unable to keep cool at the bottom. Pools deeper than 45cm (18in) tend to fill up with stagnant mud. Pools smaller than 2m by 1.25m (6ft by 4ft) are difficult to keep clear. Be generous with your dimensions.

Pool materials

Ancient craftsmen used to make pools out of puddled clay, then along came concrete. Nowadays you can do better than either of these two bulky materials, thanks to a wide range of flexible and durable pool liners.

The cheapest is undoubtedly polythene, but it also has the shortest life, usually needing renewal every two or

---

If there are unpleasant strips of concrete or lining material showing at the edge of the pool, cover them with marginal aquatics which can bridge the gap between water and land.

three years. Sunlight breaks down polythene (especially at pool rims where the liner is most exposed) eventually causing it to split, but for cheap and temporary pools polythene gives good value for money.

PVC pool liners are thicker and more expensive, but they are also longer lasting. Try to find one that has a

An informal pool with water hawthorn – see page 33

Feed water lilies once every summer by mixing a little blood, bone and fishmeal with a knub of clay soil and dropping this 'gobstopper' on to the compost in the submerged basket.

fairly muted colour, rather than that bright swimming-pool turquoise.

Fibreglass pools that look like gigantic jelly moulds might seem like an easy way out but they have several disadvantages, apart from their horrendous appearance: they are often too small and too shallow; they are usually a ghastly colour; they are always expensive.

Butyl is the best pool liner. It's a kind of reinforced rubber that has an exceptionally long life. It's black and can be bought in large sheets to make a pool of any shape. The great thing about all flexible pool liners is that you can please yourself about the design of your pool – they'll fit any shape or size.

In order of preference here's what to choose for lining your pool:

- Butyl
- PVC
- Polythene

The most desirable is also the most expensive, but it's still cheaper, per square metre (or yard) of pool surface, than most fibreglass pools.

A tub pool is ideal for a patio or tiny garden

CREATING GARDEN POOLS

Tub pools

If space is really short, make a miniature pool from half a beer barrel. Provided it's firmly held together and coated inside with a bituminous paint it will happily support a few gallons of water, a pygmy water lily (the white-flowered *Nymphaea* 'Pygmaea Alba' is best) and two or three goldfish. On your patio or terrace it will look a treat, and the fish will be blissfully happy provided you can find them a larger home in winter. Transfer them to a neighbour's pool where they won't be frozen up.

Digging the hole

There's no easy way out, unless you want to hire a JCB.

The pool will need marking out before you excavate. Canes and string can mark out formal pools; hosepipes or trails of sand snaked along the ground will show the shape of an informal pool.

Before you lift a spade, think what you're going to do with all that soil. You'll be surprised just how much earth comes out of a small hole. Don't make a heap at one end of your pool and stud it with rocks in the belief that it will look like a rock garden. To most eyes it will appear to be just what it is – a spoil heap. Try to distribute the topsoil (the dark stuff from the upper 23cm (9in) evenly over the garden, or use it to make raised beds at some distance from the pool. The subsoil (the lighter-coloured stuff that's usually poor and stony) is good for nothing except

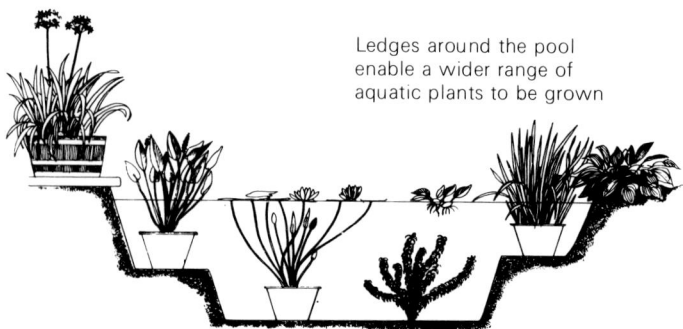

Ledges around the pool enable a wider range of aquatic plants to be grown

Stand plants such as agapanthus in terracotta pots around the rim of a formal pool. They'll look delightful during summer.

building up ground for patios and the like. Arrange for it to be carted away in a skip if you've no place for it.

Don't dig a straight-sided pool; slope the sides at an angle of about 45°. You can make one end of the pool even more gradually sloped so that birds have easy access to drink and bathe. Stepped ledges make good homes for aquatic plants that enjoy growing in the shallows.

Lining the pool

Dig out your pool gradually during late winter and early spring so that it's ready to be lined during April and planted up during May.

Calculate the size of liner you'll need as follows:

Length of pool		Width of pool
+		+
twice the depth	×	twice the depth
+		+
60cm (2ft)		60cm (2ft)

The 60cm (2ft) gives you a good flap of material to tuck in all the way round the pool (see *Edging* page 18).

Before stretching the liner over the hole and lowering it into place, check that it's not perforated. If it is; take it back and complain! Then all you need to do is:
1. Enlist the help of another pair of hands.
2. Pat the sides and bottom of the pool to ensure that they are smooth.
3. Remove any protruding stones or pieces of glass.
4. Line the hole with several thicknesses of newspaper.
5. Stretch the liner over the hole and lower it into place.
6. Anchor the edges of the liner with bricks or smooth stones.

Now the pool can be filled with water. Lay a hosepipe on the centre of the liner and turn on the tap. As the water flows in the liner will be weighed down against the sides and bottom of the pool. Ease out any severe creases if you can, otherwise they'll create weak spots.

Turn off the tap when the water has reached what you wish to be its final level.

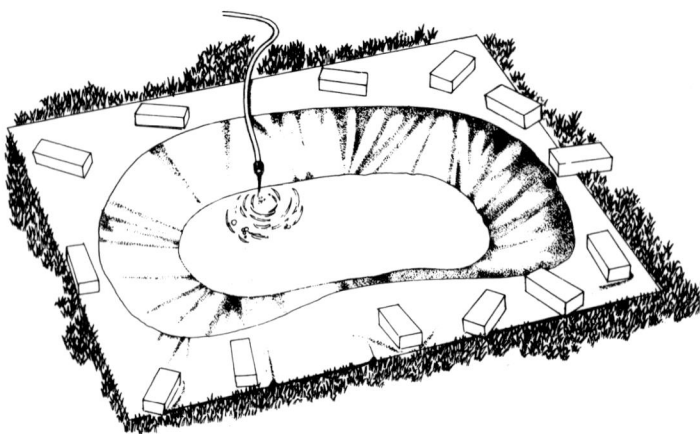

The weight of the water will press the liner into place

Edging

A pool is made or marred by its edging. The golden rule is to make sure that when the pool is full not a single piece of the liner can be seen.

The easiest way of achieving this is to edge the pool with paving slabs (crazy or square), laying them so that they overlap the rim by 2 or 3in (5 or 8cm). Firmly bedded they will produce a stable walkway around the pool which disguises the liner and prevents it from being burned by the sun.

There are alternatives to flagstones:
● Bricks
● Logs
● Turves

Bricks usually need to be mortared into place and look more 'high-tech' than slabs.

Logs can be laid on their sides, or cut into large discs and used as stepping stones, but they'll have to be anchored by soil at their outer edges if they are to be firm enough to walk on.

Turves cannot simply be laid on the liner. They'll need 10cm (4in) of soil in which to root.

Bog plants are happy growing at the side of a pool if the

Paving slabs are the most usual material with which to edge a pool

liner is taken underneath about 30cm (1ft) of soil before being brought up to the surface. Here all kinds of moisture lovers will be at home (see page 44).

One final tip: do make sure that all folded edges of the liner slope gently upwards to guard against water loss.

Strips of butyl or PVC can be used to line the lips and the channels of a waterfall. These can be masked with stone slabs to give a completely natural effect

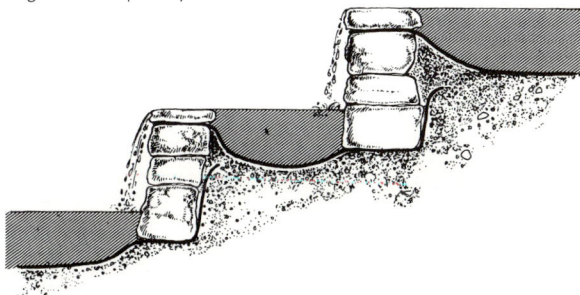

For soil in shady corners near the pool where the earth is moist but not boggy, ferns will make a verdant backdrop to the water.

If all you possess is a back yard or patio, consider a wall-mounted fountain that splashes into a shallow bowl. The effect will cool you on the hottest day.

Fountains and Features

Aquatic plants like water lilies grow best in still waters rather than raging torrents, but there's nothing to stop you having a fountain if you fancy the tinkling sound of gently playing water.

Waterfalls, too, will add movement, but for the best effect make them yourself out of real stone slabs positioned over strips of lining material; preformed plastic waterfalls will always look rather artificial.

All water features will need to be powered by a pump. The cheapest and most convenient kind to use is the submersible pump. Buy it from a garden centre or a shop that specialises in aquatic equipment. It will be quite small, encased in plastic and fitted with a short length of waterproof cable. This is the type of pump that sits below the water level and which recirculates the existing water, rather than adding fresh.

Position a submersible pump close to a waterfall otherwise disturbing currents will be caused

Check with the manufacturer's recommendations that the pump is powerful enough for your needs and that it will give you a strong enough jet for your fountain or a high enough lift for your waterfall.

Opposite: This type of elegant water feature can be fitted into the smallest patio garden or back yard

Enlist the help of a competent electrician to connect your pump to the mains. The cable will have to be taken underground at a safe depth, so it cannot be cut by a spade.

These pumps work well, and they work quietly too, but the filter should be cleaned out every few weeks to rid it of algae which impairs the pump's performance.

Floodlit pools look enchanting at night, but, again, consult an electrician before choosing and installing any outdoor lighting.

This delightful pool is surrounded by moisture-loving plants including primulas, rushes and skunks cabbage

Almost all bog plants and marginal aquatics can be propagated by division. Do the job in spring and discard any dead or weak portions before replanting the healthy bits.

CHILDREN AND WATER

If tiny tots are constantly milling around your feet, and your garden, water is a worry. It needn't be. There are ways of introducing water to the garden in such a way that it presents no safety hazard. It's the depth of water that causes problems, so find a way of creating a shallow film of water which will trickle soothingly over stone.

The millstone water feature in my own garden poses no worries as far as the children are concerned. It fascinates them and they can't leave it alone, but it won't do them any harm! It's made from an old grindstone and

My millstone water feature

attracts more attention than anything else in the garden.
Here's what you'll need to make such a feature:
- A plastic water tank (domestic) about 1m (3ft) in diameter and 75cm (2½ft) deep.
- Six concrete building blocks.
- A submersible pump plus 1m (3ft) of hosepipe and a Jubilee clip.
- A grindstone or millstone around 1m (3ft) diameter.
- A doughnut-shaped ring of butyl or plastic with an inner diameter of 75cm (2½ft) and an outer diameter of 1.25m (4ft).

- Two sacks of gravel.
- Two sacks of cobbles.
- Water and elbow grease.

Method   Dig a hole to accommodate the plastic tank. Lower it in and make sure it's firm.

Stand two concrete blocks on their edges in the bottom of the tank, then the next two at right angles on top of the first pair, and finally the last pair, again at right angles to the middle pair. You've now created a hollow column that should support the millstone 8 or 10cm (3 or 4in) above the rim of the tank.

Put the butyl or plastic ring in place so that the inner edges overlap the rim of the tank. The earth should slope towards the tank.

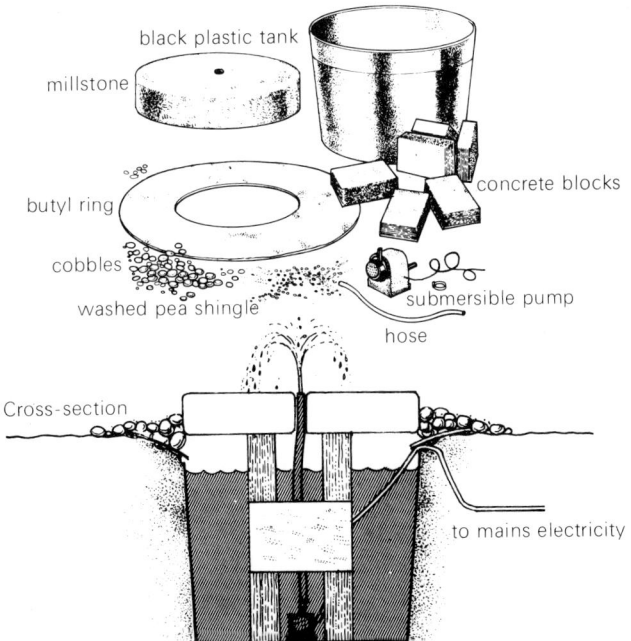

At the top is everything you need to create my millstone fountain and, below, the section shows how these materials are assembled. It really is quite simple to construct

A plastic heron 'planted' next to the pool is supposed to repel the real thing. Can you face looking at a plastic heron all the time?

Sit the millstone centrally on top of the column and make sure it's level. (Sorry! You'll need a large spirit level and another pair of hands too.) Squeeze the pump in between the stone and the rim of the tank and lower it to the bottom. (It's important that you can do this. If you can't it means lifting the stone off every time the pump needs attention, and that stone will weigh a ton – nearly.)

The cable from the pump may need to be extended; in which case have an electrician fit a weatherproof junction box. The cable can then be buried in a trench leading from the pool to the electricity supply.

There's a fiddly job to do now. A piece of hosepipe has to be fastened to the pump outlet with a Jubilee clip, and fed up through the central hole in the millstone where it is held in place with rapid setting cement. Cut off the pipe flush with the stone.

When this has been done, the tank can be filled with water to within 2 to 3in (5 to 8cm) of its rim and the pump switched on.

Water will shoot up through the centre of the stone for a height of about 15cm (6in), then it runs out across the surface, down the sides and is deflected back into the tank by the rubber ring. Adjust the level of the stone if the water refuses to cover the surface evenly.

When all is working well, surround the stone with cobbles (which will hide the rubber ring) and surround the cobbles with gravel among which foliage plants can be planted.

In winter the pump can be switched off (it can be turned off at night during the summer) but every day when the weather's pleasant the sound of running water will send you to sleep in your deck chair!

PLANTS FOR POOLS

Don't rush out to plant your pool as soon as the last drop of water trickles into it. Leave it alone for ten days or a fortnight so that the water can settle down. Then you can plant.

There are several different groups of plants that will be

happy in different parts of the pool. This is what the experts call them:

- Free-floating aquatics
- Marginal aquatics
- Fixed-floating aquatics
- Bog plants
- Submerged aquatics

Free-floating aquatics are those little plants like duckweed that bob about on the surface of the water.

Fixed-floating aquatics have leaves floating on the surface of the water, but their roots are anchored to the bottom of the pool, usually in baskets of soil. Water lilies are the most popular plants in this group.

Submerged aquatics are vital for the wellbeing of your pool. They stay below the surface giving off oxygen and keeping the water fresh. Sometimes their flowering shoots come above the surface. Fish can't live without these oxygenators.

The water lily 'Gladstoniana' – see page 36

Make a Japanese water garden by surrounding an informal pool with large pebbles and traversing it with a simple plank bridge supported on round stakes at either end.

Marginal aquatics are plants that grow with their roots in shallow water. These are the plants for the 'shelves' around your pool – like rushes and kingcups and flag irises.

Bog plants enjoy the very moisture-retentive soil that can be created at one end of the pool where the liner is taken under part of a flower bed or border. There are many of these to choose from.

How to plant

Remember that April and May are the best months for planting.

The submerged oxygenators are the easiest aquatics to plant. Tie a few stems to a pebble or a piece of lead and simply drop the weighted bunch into the water where, with any luck, it will sink to the bottom. Allow a couple of bunches to each square metre (square yard) of the pool's surface area.

Free-floating aquatics can be released on to the surface of the pool, but don't overdo them. Duckweed is best avoided altogether, for it will quickly turn your pool into a sheet of green. It's hard luck on the visitor who thinks it's a sunken lawn!

Water lilies need replanting every few years, just like other perennials. Trim any long roots before planting in fresh soil

Provide some kind of bridge or ramp between the water and the pool rim to allow young frogs to reach dry land and birds to reach the water for a drink.

Azolla, or fairy floating moss, is less rampant but needs to be overwintered in a frost-free tank indoors.

Bog plants are planted just like any other garden plant (though the earth will slurp a bit as you firm them into place).

Both marginal and fixed-floating aquatics are best planted in plastic baskets of garden soil. They can be planted in a layer of soil on the base of the pool, but fish have a tendency to stir up such mud heaps and cloud the water.

Line a plastic aquatic basket (sold especially for the purpose) with old sacking or carpet. Fill it with garden soil (rather than potting compost which contains too much fertiliser) and plant the water lily, iris or whatever in the surface after shortening any long roots. Don't plant too deeply; the roots should be just covered. Cover the surface of the soil with a layer of gravel to prevent fish from disturbing it.

Marginal aquatics can be placed straight on their shelves. Water lilies and other fixed floaters are usually stood on a couple of bricks placed in the bottom of the pool. After a couple of weeks the bricks are removed and the plants lowered to the bottom. This technique breaks them in gently.

Cover the soil in the planting basket with coarse gravel to prevent fish grubbing around and muddying the water

The variegated form of pickerel weed, *Pontederia cordata*, is a handsome marginal plant – see page 41

When clearing your pond, the displaced fish need a reserve tank with a large surface area – an old bath is ideal.

Pick of the Plants

Free-floating aquatics

Bladderwort (*Utricularia vulgaris*)
You'll find it in some freshwater pools in Britain and it's quite a talking point for the garden pool even though it may not look spectacular. The bladderwort makes a tangled mass of fine, pale green stems along which are distributed tiny pouches that supposedly capture minute forms of water life to help the plant survive. It's a sort of underwater Venus fly trap but much smaller and slower moving. Killjoys say that the pouches have nothing to do with catching prey but that they are simply buoyancy chambers. Tiny yellow snapdragons push up above the surface in summer.

Fairy floating moss (*Azolla caroliniana*)
A frilly-edged floater with pale, grey-green leaves tinged with pink. As the weather turns colder in autumn, so the pinkish tinge intensifies. The only trouble is that you'll have to fish out the plants before the frosts become too severe or they will be killed. Overwinter some of them in a fish tank indoors – they will float there happily until the weather improves the following spring and they can be put outdoors once more.

Frogbit (*Hydrocharis morsus-ranae*)
For those who love miniature plants this is a must. The leaves are like those of a water lily, but much, much smaller, and white, three-petalled flowers push up among them in summer. In autumn the plant falls to bits, and resting buds sink to the bottom of the pool to surface and grow again the following spring.

Water hyacinth (*Eichhornia crassipes*)
Although it's really a tropical plant, the water hyacinth is worth growing outdoors in summer if you can manage to keep one or two young plants going during the winter in a

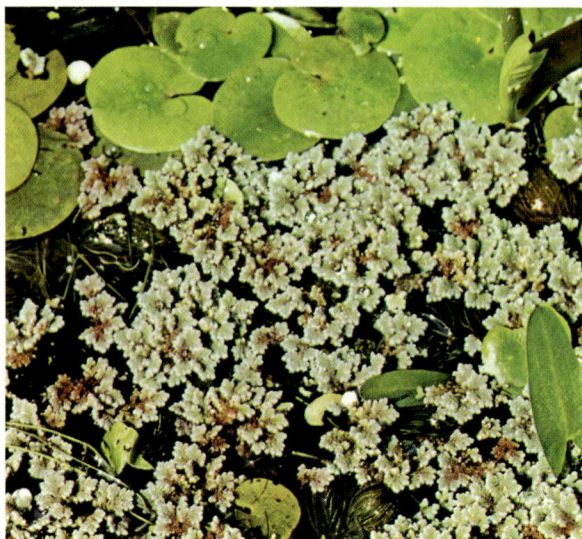

Fairy floating moss

seedpan of constantly muddy earth kept in a warm greenhouse. In tropical waterways its rate of multiplication makes it a pernicious weed; here it's never that. The large, round, glossy green leaves are slightly twisted and held on top of swollen stems that are filled with a natural foam that ensures their buoyancy. In a good summer you'll be blessed with the spectacular violet-blue flowers that are carried on short spikes. They look little like a hyacinth; far more like an orchid. A plant for the painstaking gardener!

Water soldier (*Stratiotes aloides*)
You'd think someone had dropped a pineapple top into the pool if you'd never seen the water soldier before. The spiky leaf rosettes sit below the surface of the water until summer when they surface to flower. The blooms are white and three petalled, and when the plant has done its bit it will sink below the water's surface to overwinter.

In close, muggy or stormy weather, keep the pool well oxygenated by splashing a steady trickle into the water from a hose supported 60–90cm (2–3ft) above the surface.

Fixed floating aquatics

Brandy bottle (*Nuphar lutea*)
The leaves look just like those of a water lily, floating like plates on the surface of the water, but the flowers do not. They are bright yellow and bowl shaped, and push up among the leaves in summer, each one held singly on top of a stiff stalk.

Water fringe (*Villarsia nymphaeoides*)
Also offered by some nurserymen as *Nymphoides peltata*. The leaves are like roughish versions of the water lily pad with slightly turned up margins, and the flowers that push up between them in summer look rather like those of a vegetable marrow. They are bright yellow, slightly frayed at the edges, and held singly on stalks that push them 8 or 10cm (3 or 4in) above the water.

Water fringe

Water hawthorn (*Aponogeton distachyus*)
So like the May blossom is the scent of the water hawthorn flower that it has earned this endearing common name. The leaves are large and oval and float on the surface of the water. The flowers are strangely captivating. White petals are stacked in a 'V' formation to make stout little cockades, and the soot-black spots of the anthers decorate them as they emerge in early summer. There's usually a second flush in autumn.

Water lily (*Nymphaea* species and cultivars)
No pool should be without a water lily, but don't overdo things. Too many water lily leaves turn what should be a reflective and cooling surface into a flattened mass of foliage.

All water lilies produce circular leaves of shining green, often burnished or marbled with burgundy, and they are in evidence on the water's surface for most of the year. In summer spectacular starburst blooms of white, yellow, pink, crimson or violet-blue will appear to delight you.

Water lilies come in different sizes and are best selected according to their vigour as well as their colour. Robust ones will swamp tiny pools.

Small pools
For pools up to 2m by 4m (6ft by 12ft) choose any of the following:
'Aurora' – Pads that are mottled with reddish brown and flowers that open creamy yellow, turning orange then deep red as they age.
'Comanche' – Here the flowers open pink and then become suffused with apricot until they are a rich orange-red. The leaves change colour too; opening a deep red and later becoming green.
'Froebeli' – A popular variety with flowers of a rich rosy red that are generously produced.
'Hermine' – Small flowers of great daintiness with starry petals of pure white which are set off well by the green sepals.
N. laydekeri – The hybrids of this species are ideal for pools that are of relatively modest size and with a depth of between 30 and 45cm (12 and 18in).

'Purpurata' has rich, wine-red blooms with orange anthers; 'Fulgens' is rich crimson; 'Lilacea' turns from lilac-pink to a deeper shade as it ages, and 'Alba' is pure white.
N. odorata minor – A compact lily with white flowers that is suitable for the smallest pool.
N. pygmaea – The varieties of this species comprise the

tiniest water lilies of all and they possess a grace far in excess of their size. The smallest is 'Helvola' with handsomely mottled pads that are just 5cm (2in) across; its starry flowers are pale yellow. It has a reputation for being easy to grow and apparently flowers well if grown in a bowl of water on a windowsill! 'Alba' has white flowers and 'Rubra' has pink flowers – the latter being the largest of the trio.

'Rose Arey' – One of the beefiest lilies for the small pool with very large flowers of rich pink which are freely produced.

'William Falconer' – just about the deepest red you're likely to find in a water lily.

Nymphaea marliacea 'Chromatella' is a handsome water lily for a larger pool

Don't introduce a stony stream to a modern garden; choose instead a formal, brick-edged rill – a miniature canal.

Larger pools

Where space is not so tight, and where the water is between 30 and 60cm (1 and 2ft) deep, the following varieties are among the best:

'Escarboucle' – Just about the biggest all-time favourite red, with hefty blooms of really rich, deep rose. Very free flowering.

'Gladstoniana' – A really vigorous subject with plenty of foliage (not all of which lies flat) and large white flowers. Be patient; it takes time to settle in.

'Gonnère' – Fully double white flowers. Also known as 'Crystal White' and 'Snowball' (which demonstrates just how many petals are packed into each flower).

'James Brydon' – Second only to 'Escarboucle' in the popularity stakes, and some think it better. It has really rich crimson flowers that are produced generously right through the summer.

N. marliacea – The Marliacea hybrids are among the best of all water lilies when it comes to ease of cultivation and reliable performance. 'Albida' is white; 'Carnea' is white flushed pink; 'Chromatella' is pale yellow and its leaves are marbled with reddish brown; and 'Rosea' is a touch darker in its pinkness than 'Carnea'.

'Mrs Richmond' – She's a buxom lady; her flowers are almost globular and of a rich shade of pink which deepens towards the centre.

'Rene Gerard' – If you fancy an oddity, this is the one to have. The upright-petalled flowers are pink, splashed and mottled with darker reds.

'Virginalis' – Purest white and of excellent form. The flowers have pointed petals and stand out well against the green leaves. It needs time to settle in before it flowers freely.

Submerged aquatics

A scarcity of underwater oxygenators is the cause of green water in many a pond. Make sure your pool is well supplied with some of these:

Canadian pondweed (*Elodea canadensis*)
The commonest kind of underwater 'weed' that is always

There's seldom a need to introduce frogspawn to your pool; the frogs will soon discover the breeding ground and come along to help keep down your slug population.

The water lily 'Mrs Richmond' – see opposite

sold with goldfish. The snaking stems are thickly clad in narrow green leaves that curl under. A really good oxygenator and one that multiplies well.

Curled pondweed (*Potamogeton crispus*)
Quite a handsome plant, this, with long, oval leaves that are wavy edged and often tinged with red. It branches freely but seldom becomes a real menace like some of its over-vigorous relations.

Water crowfoot (*Ranunculus aquatilis*)
An aquatic buttercup with frilly fronds of leaves under the water and proper buttercup leaves above, among which stand the white flowers in summer.

Water milfoil (*Myriophyllum* species)
Like the water crowfoot, this pond dweller has feathery underwater leaves, but it doesn't bother to produce different ones up above, instead it just sends up slender

flower spikes furnished with many-anthered but rather insignificant flowers.

Water violet (*Hottonia palustris*)
A really pretty oxygenator. Feathery, pinnate leaves appear in spring, to be followed in summer by heads of pale lilac lady's smock-type flowers on 23cm (9in) stems. They look deliciously delicate. In autumn the plant disappears, but overwintering buds sink to the bottom of the pool to regrow the following season.

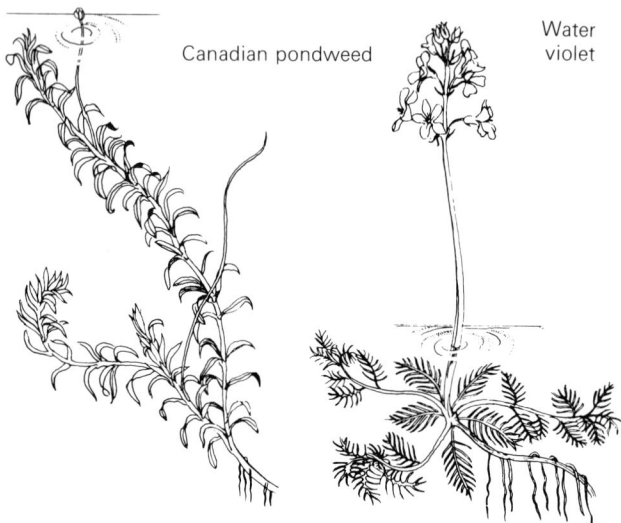

Canadian pondweed

Water violet

Marginal aquatics

Bridging the gap between deep water and the boggy rim of the pool are the so-called marginal aquatics which are usually happiest in the shallows. All of them can be propagated by division in spring.

Arrowhead (*Sagittaria sagittifolia*) 60cm (2ft)
A striking plant with a latin name that's a treat to twist your tongue round! The rich green arrowhead leaves are carried on juicy stems. It is the double-flowered form that is usually grown; this produces double white flowers on a stout stalk in summer.

Don't cover too much of the pool's surface with leaves or you'll lose the reflective properties of the water.

Arum lily (*Zantedeschia aethiopica*) 1m (3ft)
The huge arrow-shaped leaves of the arum lily will form a
stout clump, among which the waxy white flower
trumpets blow a fanfare in summer. It does display some
tenderness in winter and as a result is often grown in a
large flowerpot that can be stood on a pool shelf in
summer and removed and overwintered in a cool greenhouse. Some gardeners, though, lift the plant off the shelf
in autumn and lower it into the depths of the pool where,

The arum lily will grow in shallow water or in boggy land
close by a pool

they say, the deep water protects it. The following spring it can be raised to its summer quarters. Give any new arum a little time to settle in before expecting a wondrous show of flowers. It will need a couple of years of patience.

Bog arum (*Calla palustris*) 23cm (9in)
This baby brother of the arum lily has dark green and glossy heart-shaped leaves and miniature arum flowers of clear white. Even more spectacular are the red berries which follow the blooms in autumn. It's a good creeper; often recommended as a disguiser of the pond edge, for it sends its rhizomes from the shallow water into the moist poolside earth.

Bog bean (*Menyanthes trifoliata*) 30cm (1ft)
Three-lobed leaves, similar to those of the broad bean but a darker colour, rise above the water and in late spring are accompanied by stout stalks on which sit tiers of white,

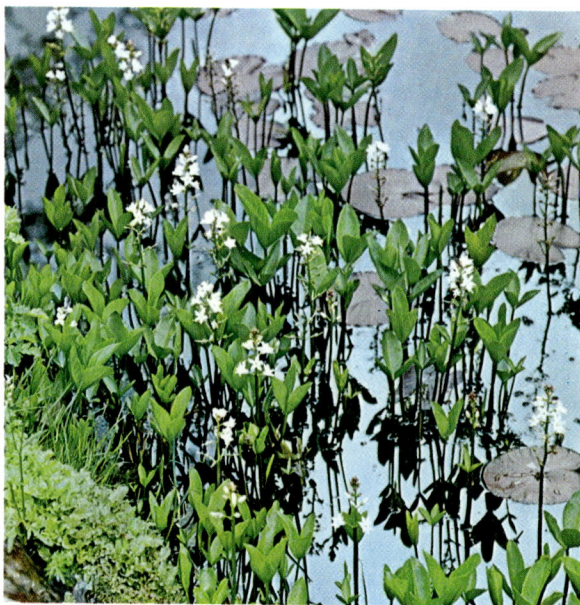

The bog bean (menyanthes)

Sink an old dustbin lid into the ground to make a drinking pool for garden birds.

fringed and frilly flowers. Another good gap bridger between water and soggy land.

Corkscrew rush (*Juncus effusus* 'Spiralis') 45cm (1½ft)
Take several green reeds, wrap them around a pair of curling tongs and you have the corkscrew rush with its quaint spiralling stems. There are no spectacular flowers, but with novel leaves like this they'd not be noticed anyway!

Flowering rush (*Butomus umbellatus*) 1m (3ft)
Here the flowers *are* more important than the leaves. The foliage is twisted and grassy and the flowers are soft pink and carried in umbrella heads on top of the long stalks in summer.

Golden club (*Orontium aquaticum*) 30cm (1ft)
The glossy green leaves of the golden club curl inwards slightly and are tightly packed across the surface of the water. Up among them push the creamy white flower stalks, tipped with bright yellow so that they look like some emaciated toadstool or the central spadix of an arum lily without the white spathe.

Kingcup (*Caltha palustris*) 30cm (1ft)
Waterblobs, we used to call them at school. The kingcup is a British native, and while it's handsome enough in its single form, the double variety 'Flore Pleno' is most usually grown in gardens. The leaves are rich green and rounded, and the early spring flowers fully double so that they look like rosettes. The whole plant has a neatness that should appeal to tidy-minded gardeners without a doubt.

Pickerel weed (*Pontederia cordata*) 45cm (1½ft)
Don't let the common name put you off growing this lovely plant. Its leaves are shiny green and arrow shaped with rounded bases, and in summer spikes of lavender blue flowers push up among them. It may not be the tidiest grower, but the blooms make up for any other shortcomings.

The golden buttercup-like flowers of *Caltha palustris*, the 'waterblob', growing by a stream

Reedmace (*Typha angustifolia*) 1.25m (4ft)
We're told not to call it the bulrush, so I won't, even though that's what most folk know it as. This is a slightly lower growing species which won't get too rampant and yet will still produce those fat brown cigar-like flower-heads on stiff stalks. Flower arrangers who find that their bulrushes turn to cotton wool after picking should try spraying them with hair lacquer.

Reed meadow grass (*Glyceria aquatica* 'Variegata') 60cm (2ft)
Although it can prove to be a real menace in the wrong place because of its amazing vigour, this grass is such a pretty plant that I'd be willing to risk it in most situations. Its fountains of leaves are striped green and white and very occasionally tinged with pink. It's happy in the water and in the moist soil at the pool edge, so let it scramble as far as you dare.

Smooth iris (*Iris laevigata*) 75cm (2½ft)
One of the prettiest irises with half a dozen wide petals that shine like bold stars from a distance. It is often confused with *Iris kaempferi* which dislikes standing in water during the winter and is therefore not such an easy plant to please. The flowers may be violet, purple, blue, rose or white, and there are also forms with variegated foliage. No pool should be without at least a couple.

Sweet flag (*Acorus calamus*) 75cm (2½ft)
The tall green iris-like leaves of the sweet flag are by no means spectacular but they exude a sweet smell when crushed and so make good conversation pieces or

Iris laevigata has dainty open flower heads and needs a lime-free soil to succeed

Keep an eye on the oxygenating plants in the pool and replace them if the fish nibble them away.

nosegays on garden strolls. The plant was once used as a strewing herb before the days of linoleum. The flowers are rather like cigars and are held out at an angle from the stems. The smaller variegated variety, at around 30cm (1ft) high, tends to get a better press than its larger relative, which is rather a shame.

Water forget-me-not (*Myosotis palustris*) 23cm (9in)
Forget-me-nots growing out of the water are a pretty sight in late spring and follow on from the fading kingcups. The leaves are unspectacular – oval and downy – but the haze of pale blue flowers is entrancing.

Water mint (*Mentha aquatica*) 45cm (1½ft)
Like the water forget-me-not, the water mint is similar in appearance to its landed relations but demands plenty of water at all times of year. The leaves are just as aromatic as those of other mints and just as useful in the kitchen. Lilac-purple flower spikes appear in summer.

Yellow flag (*Iris pseudacorus*) 1m (3ft)
Leaves like swords and bright yellow early summer flowers make the British native yellow flag a popular plant. It's dead easy to grow, too. For something a bit special try the variegated variety.

Zebra rush (*Scirpus tabernaemontanus* 'Zebrinus') 1m (3ft)
The biggest problem about this plant is the size of its latin name should you have to use it in the nursery. Its unique appearance makes perseverance worthwhile for it produces porcupine quills that are alternatively banded with bright green and cream.

Bog plants

Lots of garden plants demand a soil that never dries out however hard the sun beats down in summer. The rim of a pool, where the surrounding soil can draw water from the reservoir as it needs it, offers them just the conditions they need.

Bleeding heart (*Dicentra spectabilis*) 45cm (1½ft)
In early spring the feathery grey-green foliage pushes up
from the ground and over the top of it in May are held
gently arching stems from which dangle perfectly formed
heart-shaped lockets of rich pink. There is a white variety
'Alba' which is especially fashionable and just as easy to
grow. Both look breathtakingly beautiful when their
lockets dangle over a sheet of water.

Candelabra primulas and the yellow variegated form of *Iris pseudacorus*

Snails are not necessary in a garden pool. Don't bother with
them.

Bugle (*Ajuga* species and varieties) 15cm (6in)
Trouble-free little carpeters with spires of blue flowers in spring. However, nowadays it's the leaves that are the main attraction, for there are varieties with all manner of coloured markings. 'Variegata' is marbled green, cream and pink; 'Multicolor' is a psychedelic confection of deep purple, red and orange, and 'Burgundy Glow' is a mixture of cream and carmine that intensifies in its rosiness as the cold weather approaches. All make thick, weed-suppressing rugs and spread rapidly.

Cardinal flower (*Lobelia cardinalis*) 1m (3ft)
Although its a good deal grander than its dwarf relation so often used in tandem with white alyssum, the resemblance between this lobelia and its summer-bedding relation can be noticed in the shape of the flowers. The leaves of the plant are narrow and green, the flower stems are tall and stately, and the flowers, carried in spikes, are rich scarlet. One of the most imposing waterside plants.

Creeping jenny (*Lysimachia nummularia*) 5cm (2in)
The plain green creeping jenny can be found in British woodlands, but it is the yellow-leaved form 'Aurea' that is most frequently grown in gardens. It still carries the small yellow cup-shaped flowers and spreads fast in moist ground to make a yellow blanket.

Day lily

A clump of aquatic irises sunk into the water will provide egg-laying sites for handsome dragonflies.

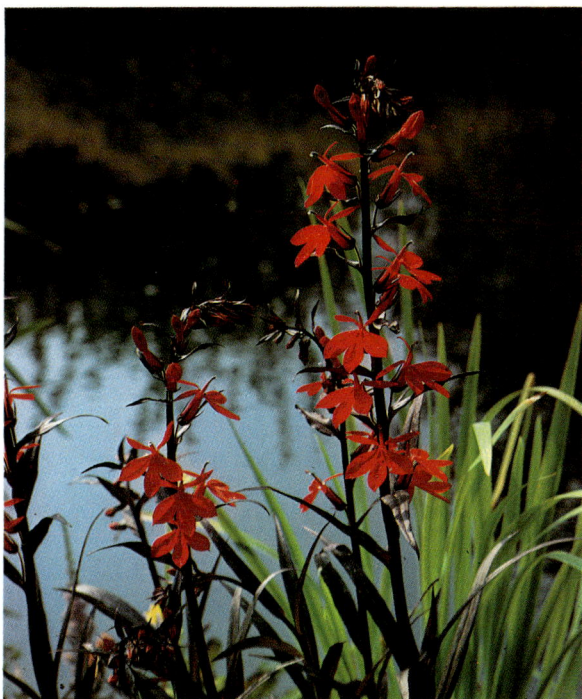

Lobelia cardinalis is a stately plant with flowers of the richest shade of scarlet

Day lily (*Hemerocallis* species and varieties) 1m (3ft)
The huge clumps of bright green grassy leaves show off well the sprays of lily-like flowers, each of which lasts for a single summer's day. But plenty of blooms are produced so the plant has a long season of flowering. Varieties are offered with yellow, pink, white, orange, red and deep mahogany flowers, and there are dwarf varieties for small gardens.

Globe flower (*Trollius europaeus*) 60cm (2ft)
The dark green leaves of the globe flower are fingered and make a rounded mound through which push golden orbs of bloom in spring. It's a sort of large-flowered, up-market buttercup.

Goat's beard (*Aruncus sylvester*) 1.25m (4ft)
The goat's beard is really a huge spirea with finely cut, almost ferny foliage, and huge frothy plumes of creamy white flowers. It needs a bit of elbow room but really does earn its keep when the blooms open in early summer.

Iris 75cm (2½ft)
Not all irises like really boggy ground, but two in particular revel in it. *Iris sibirica* makes a mass of narrow green leaves and over the top of these tower elegant stems of beautifully marked blue, purple or white flowers. It must be one of the most statuesque garden irises. *Iris kaempferi* is larger flowered and available in a greater variety of colours, from blue through violet to maroon, white and pink, often contrastingly blotched. It's not too keen on being kept soggy in winter, so planting it a little higher than the water's surface will help ensure its survival.

Lady's mantle (*Alchemilla mollis*) 45cm (1½ft)
The leaves are downy and scalloped at the edges and they hold droplets of water as though they were diamonds. The frothy, foaming flowers of lime green billow over the leaves in summer. Snip them off before they set seed unless you want to be overrun by seedlings. Good ground cover.

Lady's smock (*Cardamine pratensis*) 30cm (1ft)
The cuckoo flower is a welcome herald of spring on ditch-sides countrywide, and its double form 'Flore Pleno' is a little cracker of a garden plant with pale lilac flowers rather like those of a ten-week stock. They last well, too, and look especially good when associated with the blooms of dark purple violas.

Ligularia 1.25m (4ft)
I've resisted using the common name of golden groundsel lest it should give the plant a bad name. It's a beefy monster with coarse, heart-shaped leaves and branched flowerheads that carry deep yellow daisies. It makes a welcome statuesque change from the fussiness of other

waterside plants. Several varieties are available with blooms that vary in colour intensity.

Loosestrife (*Lythrum salicaria*) 1m (3ft)
The tall, rich pink spires of loosestrife are doubly welcome in the garden for they open in mid- to late summer when most other flowers have been doing their bit for some time. The leaves are narrow and green and the spires quite long. Several varieties are sold and they vary in their intensity of colour. 'Firecandle' is one of the best.

Meadowsweet (*Filipendula ulmaria*) 1m (3ft)
Grow the plain green meadowsweet if you especially want to, but brighter-leaved is the golden form 'Aurea' with acid yellow, pinnate leaves. The flowers are white and frothy and open in early to midsummer.

Monkey flower (*Mimulus* species and varieties) 30cm (1ft)
The shiny green leaves of the monkey flower are topped in summer with sheets of musk flowers that may be yellow, orange or red, often brightly spotted like some exotic reptile. They are easy to raise from seed and will

A pretty little raised pond with rounded coping – so comfortable to sit on, no sharp edges

Netting stretched over the pool from early autumn until early winter will catch all falling leaves and prevent them from fouling the water.

usually keep themselves going at the waterside by sowing their own.

Ornamental rhubarb (*Rheum palmatum*) 2m (6ft) or more
It comes as something of a shock to the uninitiated to find rhubarb growing next to the garden pool, but this species is rather more handsome than the culinary variety with leaves that are deeply cut and flushed with deepest crimson. 'Atrosanguineum' is the variety with the reddest flower spike that towers well above the giant mound of leaves.

An informal pond in a rocky setting features hostas, variegated iris and the golden form of creeping jenny

If fishing cats are a problem give them a squirt from a water-filled detergent bottle; it usually puts them off for a few days.

Plantain lily (hosta) produces spikes of white or pale mauve flowers in summer

Plantain lily (*Hosta* species and varieties) Up to 75cm (2½ft)
There are now so many different hostas that a society has been devoted to them, along with their poolside companions the day lilies (hemerocallis). The oval, juicy leaves may be plain green, variegated with white, cream or yellow, or glaucous blue, and the flowers that are held in spikes above them may be white or pale lilac. All are worth growing in moist soil but they must be protected from slugs when their leaves unfurl in spring.

Prickly rhubarb (*Gunnera manicata*) 2.5m (8ft)
Not for small plots. Gigantic rhubarb leaves on tall stalks that can provide welcome shelter from summer showers. The stalks and the undersides of the leaves carry hard spines which make the application of custard undesirable. The flowers are rather like bizarre pine cones that appear at ground level. It needs a protective blanket of straw or bracken when the leaves have died down in autumn, and a constant supply of water.

Primula (Candelabra types) Up to 75cm (2½ft)
There are lots of different candelabra primulas, which derive their common name from the fact that their dainty flowers are carried in tiers upon the flower stem. The

Rodger's bronze leaf and candelabra primulas in flower together in early summer

blooms of white, yellow, orange, pink or red may open from late spring to midsummer. *P. bulleyana*, orange; *P. japonica*, purplish red, and *P. pulverulenta*, purplish red with stems coated in white meal, are especially good, as is the pale yellow *P. sikkimensis* with its dock-like leaves and top-knot of pendulous sulphur yellow flowers. The 'Harlow Car Hybrids' are about the best mixture of colours.

Rodger's bronze leaf (*Rodgersia aesculifolia*) 1m (3ft)
There are a number of rodgersias widely available, but this is one of the best. It has bronzed, horse-chestnut-shaped leaves, and stiff plumes of pinkish cream flowers in late spring and early autumn.

Skunk cabbage (*Lysichitum* species) 1m (3ft)
I shouldn't really use this common name which strictly speaking belongs to another plant, but then in common usage it is most frequently applied to the two lysichitums — *L. americanum*, with yellow arum flowers, and *L. camtschatcense*, with white arum flowers, in spring. In both cases the blooms appear from the soggy mud before the leaves, which are gigantic things that look as though they are made of green leather. Give them a fair bit of space.

Spiraea (*Astilbe* varieties) 75cm (2½ft)
No poolside or streamside planting would be complete without astilbes and their tapering plumes of white, pink or red flowers, set off well against the ferny foliage that's often burnished purple. If space is short try the dwarf variety 'Sprite' with pink plumes. It grows just 30cm (1ft) high.

Yellow loosestrife (*Lysimachia punctata*) 60cm (2ft)
The spikes of yellow starry flowers on the yellow loosestrife open in summer on a plant that makes broad clumps. So easily does it spread that it can become a nuisance. Plant it where it can do no harm to its neighbours.

Fish and a fountain enliven this pool. Thickly-planted margins give a natural effect

FISH

It's a shame to have a pool without fish in it. You'll have plenty of dingy-coloured inhabitants in the form of frogs and toads, so you might just as well introduce some brighter-coloured wildlife.

Wait until the aquatic plants are well established in the pool; introduce your fish about two months after planting, in June or July when the water's warm.

Golden orfe are the best fish if you fancy gazing on pale orange shoals that cruise just below the surface, but they can't match the common goldfish for brilliance. Both are

Introduce fish carefully into their new home

quite hardy when it comes to spending winters outdoors, and they'll grow at a rate of knots.

Koi carp are for the enthusiast. They're very expensive and often marbled in quite revolting colours! Goldfish represent far better value for money.

Buying fish   Buy your fish from a reputable pet shop and choose only those that are lively and free from white strands of fungus that can cripple them. (Mind you, fish won at fairgrounds have survived for years with me!)

Don't cram too many fish into your pool. Allow at least 30 cm sq (1 sq ft) of surface area for each fish. Bring the fish home in a well-wrapped polythene bag which should be suspended in the pool for an hour or two before the fish are released. This allows the temperature of the water in the bag to equalise gradually with that in the pool, so preventing the fish from having a shock to their systems.

Fish do need feeding during the summer. Pellets are best and can be scattered in the pool once a week from April to September. Allow one pellet per fish. Some folk recommend more; my fish have always survived, and grown, on this somewhat spartan diet. Don't feed the fish in winter; they don't need it as their metabolism slows down to a snail's pace.

A rock garden provides a perfect backdrop for this pool

PROBLEM PAGES

Green water   This is the commonest problem in garden pools. Every new pond is going to turn green within a few days of being filled. Equipped with plenty of oxygenating plants, and made to the correct dimensions, it will eventually clear. Occasional 'pea-soupers' may occur each spring, but that's only to be expected with the advent of warm weather. Don't, whatever you do, change the water or the process will start all over again. Pools which refuse to settle down, and which are constantly green are probably too shallow.

Blanket weed (those long, green strands) may appear regularly, but it can be easily (and very satisfyingly) pulled out with a wire-toothed garden rake.

Herons   There's little you can do to stop these elegant birds from plundering your pool and spearing the fish for their dinner. Green plastic netting stretched over the surface will deter them, but then who wants to look at plastic netting? If repeated attacks occur you may just have to do without fish.

Cats   Cats are less of a problem. Spot them fishing and creep up on them. Pushed into the water a couple of times they'll soon discover more profitable ways of hunting for lunch.

Fish ailments   There are all sorts of fish diseases, most of which you'll never see, but one in particular crops up more frequently than the rest. It's called white fungus. The fish become listless and develop white strands on their bodies. It's possible to cure the disease by removing the affected fish and isolating them for several weeks in a bowl of chemically treated water. The fish look miserable and don't always pull round. It's often as well to put them out of their misery at the start. It sounds cruel, but at least it's a quick death.

Pool cleaning   Don't do it very often. If the pool does become rather tatty looking, clean it out every other spring. Siphon out the water and shovel out the mud in the bottom. You can take the opportunity of giving aquatic plants a fresh basket of soil at the same time, dividing up

Sickly fish are best removed from the pool and disposed of as soon as they are seen and before infection spreads. It sounds cruel but is safer in the long term.

large clumps and throwing away the worn-out portions. Oh, and do remember to remove the fish and put them in a bucket of pond water *before* you start the clean-up.

Remember to top up your garden pool regularly in hot sunny weather. This arrangement helps oxygenate the water

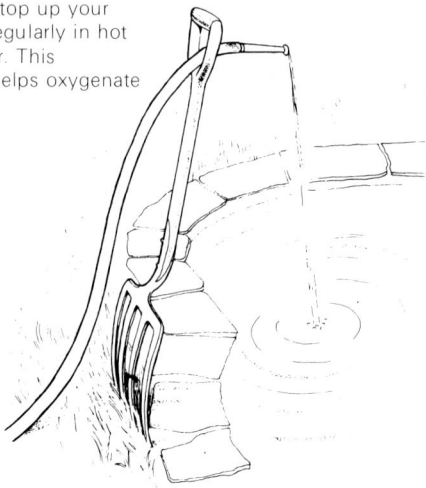

Topping up Bright and sunny summer weather will cause water to evaporate from the pool. Top it up from a hosepipe to keep it full and to prevent the edges of the liner from being exposed to sunlight.

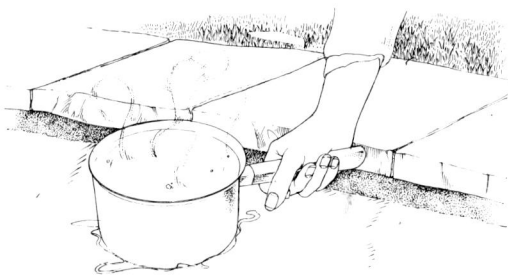

Remember to give fish a breathing hole when your pond is frozen over. Never break the icy by hammering, though, as this will give rise to harmful shock waves

Fish need to breathe in winter but ice prevents them from doing so. Stand a pot of hot water on the ice to melt a hole and allow in oxygen.

INDEX